PROFILES · IN · MUSIC

Mozart

LIBRARY OF CONGRESS CATALOGING-IN-PUBLICATION DATA

Loewen, Nancy, 1964-
    Mozart / by Nancy Loewen.
        p. cm. -- (Profiles in music)
    Includes index.
    Summary: Follows the life of the talented Austrian composer, from his performances as a child prodigy to his early death and burial in an unmarked pauper's grave.
    ISBN 0-86592-605-0
    1. Mozart, Wolfgang Amadeus, 1756-1791--Juvenile literature. 2. Composers--Austria--Biography--Juvenile literature.
[1. Mozart, Wolfgang Amadeus, 1756-1791. 2. Composers.]
I. Title. II. Series: Loewen, Nancy, 1964-   Profiles in music.
ML3930.M9L64 1989
780' .92--dc20   89-32263
[B]   CIP
                                                        AC MN

© 1989 Rourke Enterprises, Inc.

PROFILES · IN · MUSIC

Mozart

TEXT BY
NANCY LOEWEN

**DESIGN & PRODUCTION BY
MARK E. AHLSTROM
(The Bookworks)**

ROURKE ENTERPRISES, INC.
Vero Beach, FL 32964
U.S.A.

WOLFGANG AMADEUS MOZART
1756-1791

TABLE OF CONTENTS

CREDITS

PHOTOS AND ILLUSTRATIONS

FPG Int'l. .... cover photo, 4, 69

Jason Hailey/FPG 57

Bernard G. Silberstein/FPG ....
.... 58-59

Eric M. Sanford/FPG 60

Photoworld/FPG 61, 62-63,
.... 65, 66-67

Photo From European/FPG 64

K. Reinhard/FPG 68

TYPESETTING AND LAYOUT: THE FINAL WORD
PRINTING: WORZALLA PUBLISHING CO.

Wolfgang Amadeus Mozart: A Musical Genius

The audience in the great opera house in Vienna is getting restless. Men tug at their powdered wigs and twiddle with the buttons on their jackets. Women, dressed in fancy gowns, stir uncomfortably in their seats. Tonight, May 1, 1786, is the premiere of the opera *The Marriage of Figaro*. But some premiere! The singers seem to be purposely messing up their lines. The orchestra is flat and dull.

At last the curtain falls at the end of the first act. The confused audience sighs in relief.

Wolfgang Amadeus Mozart, the opera's composer and conductor, is sitting at the piano. His small face is pinched with worry and anger. He wipes his sweaty palms on his coat. What a terrible evening this has become!

He'd had problems with this opera from the

very beginning. It was based on a French play that was banned from the German theater in Vienna, probably because it poked fun at the nobility. His partner, Lorenzo da Ponte, had written the text for the opera. Lorenzo had worked hard changing the scenes that were most likely to offend the upper classes. Still, da Ponte had a tough time getting permission from the emperor to put on the opera.

To top that off, the court musicians were jealous of Mozart's abilities. The worst one was the court composer, an Italian man named Salieri. Salieri had tried to convince the Emperor that Mozart couldn't write an opera worthy of the Viennese people. Then Salieri and a man named Count Rosenberg had tried to stir up still more trouble at the rehearsals. Now, it seemed, even the singers had been persuaded to bungle their lines. These jealous musicians would stop at nothing to ruin Mozart!

Sitting miserably at the piano, Mozart tries to gather his courage. Finally he approaches Emperor Joseph. He reaches to kiss the emperor's hand, as is the custom. Looking at Mozart's face, the emperor can guess what has happened. He turns to Count Rosenberg, who is sitting next to him.

"Go tell those singers to sing this opera as they should!" Emperor Joseph orders in a loud voice. "Otherwise they shall all leave my service this very night!"

Rosenberg slinks away and does as the emperor has commanded.

The curtain rises for the second act. The people in the audience settle down and brace themselves for a very long evening. After just a few moments, however, the embarrassing first act is forgotten. A change has taken place! The actors are energetic, and their characters are strong. The singing is perfectly in tune. The orchestra plays beautifully—and such music! The crowd begs for encores after nearly every number. After the curtain falls on the final act, they call out, "Mozart! Mozart! Mozart!" The applause goes on and on.

Grinning from ear to ear, 29-year-old Wolfgang Amadeus Mozart happily bows before the audience. He thinks to himself, "Maybe now I'll get an appointment to the court. Maybe *Figaro* will finally turn things around for me."

As he enjoys the glory of the moment, Mozart cannot know that his hopes for the future will not come true. Yes, he will eventually receive a post with the court, but it will bring him neither the acclaim nor the financial security he has spent his life searching for. Even the Viennese people will soon forget this magnificent night.

In the end, *Figaro*—to this day one of the greatest operas ever written—was to Mozart but an empty triumph.

• • •

Wolfgang Amadeus Mozart, an Austrian, was one of the most important composers of the classical period. The classical period lasted from about 1750 to 1820. During this time, musicians paid special attention to the balance and contrast between the different parts of a musical work. Most music was light and elegant. Audiences could enjoy it easily. Two other famous composers during this time were Franz Joseph Haydn and Ludwig van Beethoven.

Mozart began his musical career as a very young child. In fact, he is considered one of the most amazing examples of child prodigy that the world has ever known. But it was as an adult that Mozart made a lasting contribution to musical history. He wrote more than 600 compositions, including operas, symphonies, sonatas, and church music. His music is still performed all across the world, nearly two hundred years after his death.

Although Mozart was respected for his musical talents during his lifetime, he was not recognized as being a musical genius. To the people of that time, he was just another musician—better than most, but not one of the "greats." Few people would have guessed that Mozart's music would survive into the 20th century.

Maybe it took musical genius to recognize his talent. Mozart did get praise from other important composers. As a young boy he studied with Johann Christian Bach, son of the great Johann Sebastian Bach. Ludwig van Beethoven, as a teenager, approached Mozart for music lessons. He wanted to learn from a master! And Franz Joseph Haydn once told Mozart's father, "I, as an honest man, tell you before God that your son is the greatest composer I know in person and by name."

Mozart was a small, plain man. His lively sense of humor, however, won him many friends—and more than a few disapproving enemies. He was careless with money when he had it, and spent most of his adult life juggling debts. His days alternated between working to exhaustion and enjoying carefree moments whenever he possibly could.

The intensity of Mozart's life caught up with him in the winter of 1791, when he died at the age of 35. Buried in an unmarked pauper's grave, he left behind a widow, two young sons, and many unpaid debts.

More importantly, Wolfgang Amadeus Mozart left behind a collection of wonderful music that the world will always treasure.

1 CHAPTER — A CHILD PRODIGY

"These are wonder children!"

—Visitors' comments after hearing
Mozart and his sister play the clavier

The Setting

At the time of Mozart's birth, present-day Austria was part of the Holy Roman Empire. This was an organization of European territories that had existed for hundreds of years. Ruling over these territories was the Holy Roman Emperor, who lived in Vienna.

During this period, Austria was divided into city-states. Each city-state was ruled by a prince. Some princes were also electors, which meant that they helped choose the Holy Roman Emperor.

The rulers of the city-states set up their courts as richly as they could. Each court had a *Kappellmeister* (concert master) who was in charge of all music performed in the area. These people oversaw the music for churches, as well as for special events such as festivals and balls. Most musicians dreamed of becoming a Kappellmeister.

Mozart's father, Leopold, was the Vice-Kappellmeister in Salzburg, a small city in what is now the nation of Austria. Leopold was also a court composer and performer. He played many instruments, including the organ, violin, and clavier. (The clavier was a general name for any stringed keyboard instrument, such as the harpsichord and piano.) Leopold gave music lessons, too, and even wrote a very popular book about violin playing.

Leopold was married to Anna Maria Bertlin, the daughter of a court official. Like many women of that time, she let her husband make most of the household decisions. Her task was to tend to her family and home. Although she was not musically gifted, she loved to sing light-hearted songs. Her cheerfulness and sense of humor made their home cozy and peaceful.

Nothing could have pleased Leopold more than to have children who loved music as much as he did. In the 18th century, families usually had lots of children, but many of them died soon after birth. In six years, Anna gave birth to six children. Only one of them, a girl, survived.

Then the Mozarts had another child. Leopold's dearest wish was about to come true—and then some!

Wolfgang Amadeus Mozart was born in Salzburg on January 27, 1756. The day after he was born, the family bundled up the tiny baby in the warmest clothes they could find. They took him out in the bitterly cold day to the Salzburg Cathedral. There he was christened in the Catholic tradition. Mozart, like most children of that time, was given a very long name. He was christened Johan Chrysostom Wolfgang Theophilus Mozart. Later he used the Latin version of Theophilus instead, which is Amadeus. His family fondly nicknamed him "Wolferl."

A Musical Family

Mozart's early years were happy ones. The family lived on the third floor of a tall, narrow house. It was near the court chapel where Leopold worked. Across the street was an open square with a beautiful fountain. Inside the house, plants lined the windows. Herr Canari, their pet bird, chirped noisily from his cage to anyone who would listen. The family dog was always ready for fun.

Naturally, music was very important in the Mozart house. Instruments and sheets of music were everywhere. Musician friends often stopped by to play the latest compositions, as well as the old favorites. The young Mozart had a good friend in his sister, Anna Maria. She was nearly five years older than he was. Nannerl, as she was called, was musically talented, too. She started taking clavier lessons from her father when she was still a little girl. Sometimes when Nannerl was practicing, Mozart would drop all his toys. As if in a trance, he'd walk over to the clavier. Standing very still, he would stare and stare at the instrument.

One day, after Nannerl had finished her lesson for the day, three-year-old Mozart toddled over to the clavier. He grabbed some pillows and put them on the seat so that he would be tall enough to see the keyboard. He started touching the keys. Soon he discovered two notes that sounded pretty when they were played together. He searched all over the keyboard for more keys that would make the same kind of sound.

His family came rushing in from the next room. They looked at him in surprise. Nannerl hugged her little brother. "Look at this!" she exclaimed. "Wolferl is only three, and he's already discovered the thirds!"

Young Mozart just smiled at them and kept on playing more pairs of keys.

Early Lessons

By the time Mozart turned four, his father had started giving him lessons on the clavier, just like his sister. Nannerl was a very good player. But Mozart seemed to know everything before he was even taught. After practicing just a short while, he could play a difficult minuet almost perfectly. Leopold took this sign of his son's talent very seriously. He began each lesson with a prayer, believing that his son's genius was a gift from God. Leopold felt it was his duty to guide Mozart's talent as best he could.

Before long Mozart was not only playing well,

but also creating new music. He would often make up songs on the clavier, and Leopold would write them down. One of these pieces, "Minuet in G," is still played today.

Soon the young boy was even writing down his compositions by himself.

One Thursday night, Leopold brought a friend to the house. Herr Schachtner was the court trumpeter. The two men discovered five-year-old Mozart surrounded by his father's music paper. He was busily writing down his latest composition. Absorbed by what he was doing, he was dipping his pen too far into the ink pot. Ink was everywhere! It was smeared all over the paper, and on Mozart's little face and hands, too.

Leopold didn't scold his son for making a mess. Instead he asked Mozart in a serious voice what he has working on.

"Oh, it's a concerto for the clavier," Mozart replied, hardly looking up from his work. "The first part is almost finished!"

The men smiled and exchanged glances. Finally Leopold convinced Mozart to let him see it.

As Leopold studied the piece, two tears fell slowly down his face. Underneath all the ink blots and smears was a score for a concerto. It was almost too difficult to play, but it was very good music.

In love with music of all kinds, it wasn't long before Mozart wanted to try something new. "Please, Papa, get me a violin!" he begged his father. Leopold soon got a tiny violin for his son. He just couldn't say no to anything having to do with music.

Shortly after Mozart got his new instrument, a group of his father's friends were at the house. They were going to play some new violin trios. "Can I play second violin?" Mozart pestered his father. "Please, Papa?" But Leopold didn't want Mozart to play. His son hadn't had any formal violin lessons yet. Finally, though, he gave in. "All right," Leopold sighed. "Just be sure not to play very loud." To everyone's astonishment, Mozart played the part perfectly.

But Mozart didn't like all instruments. Until he was 10 years old, he was terribly afraid of the sounds made by brass instruments, such as trumpets and horns. They weren't so scary when they were played with other instruments, but hearing them alone sent Mozart into a panic. Leopold wanted his son to get over this childish fear. One day he convinced his friend, Herr Schachtner, to play his trumpet in front of Mozart. As Schachtner later wrote, "Almost as soon as Wolfgang heard it, he turned pale and began to reel. If I had continued any longer, he would certainly have fallen into convulsions."

On his own, Mozart overcame this strange fear. Eventually he learned to love the brass instruments.

Testing the Waters

Friends of the family were stopping by more and more often. They wanted to hear Mozart and Nannerl perform. "These are wonder children!" the amazed guests would exclaim. Anna Maria and Leopold would stand to the side, beaming with pride, as the children played.

Leopold started thinking. What if he took his wonder children on the road, to play for the nobility? Mozart and Nannerl wouldn't be young forever. And as they grew older, their talent would seem ordinary. Maybe, if enough important people saw them now, they would find a rich patron to support the children. Having a patron was the only way in those days for musicians and other artists to make a living and become known. Patrons paid musicians to write music and to perform.

With this in mind, Leopold arranged a short trip to Munich, the capital of Bavaria. The prince there had an elaborate court. Many wealthy noblemen lived in the area. And it would soon be the carnival season, or *Fasching*. This was the time from Christmas to Lent when all sorts of festivities took place—operas, concerts, masked balls, and parties. What better time to introduce his wonder children to the world!

In order to perform in any city, musicians first had to be invited to give a concert for the reigning prince. Then they could give other performances in private houses and palaces. Leopold had a knack for public relations. It didn't take him long to arrange several concerts in Munich. "Mama," he told his wife, "start getting the children ready!"

Anna Maria brushed their warmest coats for the trip. She polished buckles and buttons, and even knitted some warm stockings and mittens for her family. The children weren't one bit scared of the great adventure awaiting them. "When do we go?" Mozart kept asking. "Oh, I can't wait!"

At last, in January 1762, Leopold, Nannerl, and Mozart set out on their trip. It was a great success. When Nannerl and Mozart played the clavier and violin, the people of Munich listened with dropped jaws. These small children could play better than most adults! They were especially taken with six-year-old Mozart. His fingers barely reached the keys. His legs didn't touch the floor. Yet, at the request of the audience, this young child could play the clavier while blindfolded. He could even play when its keys were covered with a cloth!

Mozart and Nannerl didn't let all the attention

go to their heads. They knew they still had a lot to learn. This impressed the people of Munich even more, for the children had such natural manners. They weren't one bit spoiled or rude. They gave concert after concert, always delighting their audiences. Mozart loved performing. He also learned to watch the audience, and could soon tell which people were really interested in music and which ones were just following the crowd.

But the highlight of the trip was when Leopold took them to see an Italian opera. Mozart sat very still during the performance. Afterwards, he said, "Papa, someday I'm going to write a great opera, too!"

After three weeks of nearly constant perform-ing, it was time to go home again. Leopold was very pleased. He was convinced that under his guid-ance, his children—especially Wolferl—would bring the family fame and riches.

Performing for the Emperor

Back in Salzburg, Mozart and Nannerl busily practiced their music. They also studied other subjects, including French, Italian, and history. Public schools didn't exist then. Only the rich could afford to send their children to private schools. So Leopold taught his children himself in their home. Anna Maria helped out, too.

The family was already looking forward to another trip—this time to Vienna! Vienna was the home of the emperor. Since the twelfth century, Vienna had been known as "the city of music." Leopold decided that it would be the perfect place for his children's next performances. "Surely I can find a patron in Vienna," he thought.

In September 1762, the family set out once more. This time Anna Maria came along, too, because they were going to be away for a long time. They tied their carefully wrapped instruments to the roof of the coach Leopold hired. The family rode in the coach to the town of Linz. Then they took a mail-boat down the beautiful Danube River to Vienna.

At last they arrived in the city of music. Almost before they knew it, they were given a command to perform for the royal court. Anna Maria rushed around, curling the children's hair, polishing their shoes and buttons, and scrubbing their faces. The Imperial Carriage—with its gold trim and plush red seats—was sent to bring the family to the palace. The children were very excited as they pulled up at the entrance.

A footman took the family to see the emperor. They walked through room after room of high ceilings, gleaming floors, and sparkling chandeliers. With every step Leopold and Anna Maria grew more nervous. Mozart and Nannerl just got more excited, looking in awe at the beautiful palace.

Mozart liked Empress Maria Theresa right away. After Nannerl made her finest curtsey to the royal family, Mozart bowed as Leopold had taught him. Then suddenly he climbed into the empress' lap! He threw his arms around her neck and give her a good, hard kiss. Leopold ducked his head. How embarrassing! But everyone else just laughed. They were charmed by the little boy, and by the sweet Nannerl, too.

The concert went so well that the Mozart children were invited back to give several more performances. Emperor Francis I chatted with Mozart often, calling him "the little wizard." But Mozart didn't like the emperor as much as he liked the empress. The emperor was more interested in Mozart's tricks than in the music itself.

"See if you can play with just one finger," the Emperor challenged one day. To everyone's amazement, Mozart did just that. Although he resented doing this kind of trick, he was always polite and did as he was asked. Later, as a grown man, he'd get very angry at such requests.

Mozart and Nannerl had a lot of fun playing with the royal children. One day they were running through the long palace halls when Mozart slipped on the polished floor. The little princess Marie Antoinette helped him to his feet. Mozart liked the way the princess treated him. "You are a good girl," he told Marie solemnly. "When I grow up I'm going to marry you."

Although the Mozarts were invited guests of the royalty, musicians who were not from noble families were still considered lower-class people. They ranked only a little above the servants. That's why it came as a great surprise when the empress decided to give the children a special present. She had some costumes made that looked just like the clothes the royal children wore. Mozart's costume was a purple silk coat decorated with gold braiding. Nannerl's was a white taffeta dress with fancy embroidery. In those days, children wore clothes that were exact copies of the clothes that grown-ups wore.

Throughout Vienna, the word spread that the Mozart children were wonderfully talented. Soon they had more invitations to perform than Leopold could have imagined. They gave as many as three concerts in one day! All the running from one place to another, however, soon became too much. Exhausted, the young Mozart caught scarlet fever. For two weeks he couldn't get out of his bed.

Mozart's illness was a stroke of bad luck. The nobles lost interest in the wonder children. They were afraid of contagious diseases. Even after Mozart was well, invitations to perform were fewer and fewer. At last Leopold decided to go back to Salzburg. He was a little angry at how quickly the nobility forgot about them.

The Vienna trip didn't end as Leopold had hoped. He had again failed to find a patron for his children, and would have to try somewhere else. Overall, though, the trip was successful. They'd received invitations to go to Paris and Versailles in France. And they'd made enough money to finally buy their own carriage. Now they wouldn't have to hire one when they needed to go somewhere. Mozart loved the new carriage. It could go very fast!

THE GRAND TOUR

2 | CHAPTER

"No young child could possibly play so well!"

**—jealous musicians in London who insisted
that Mozart was really older than he claimed**

New
Adventures

In June 1763, the musical Mozart family set out for France. In order to make the trip, Leopold had taken a long leave of absence from his position at the Salzburg court. This was a common practice. In those days, musicians were expected to travel.

Anna Maria didn't like to leave their peaceful, sunny home. She would miss her friends and the familiar buildings of Salzburg. But Mozart and Nannerl didn't mind leaving their home again. They were used to life on the road. It was hard work, but they got to see so many interesting places and people. About the only thing they didn't like was saying good-bye to their pets. A maid would be looking after them while the family was away. "Good-bye, Herr Canari!" Mozart called out as their new carriage started rolling away.

On the very first day of their trip, a back wheel on the carriage broke. They had to stop for a few days in the little town of Wasserburg to get the wheel fixed. Leopold fussed and fretted about the delay, but it turned out to be a good thing.

To pass time, Leopold took Mozart into a church to show him the big pipe organ. After watching his father play, Mozart announced, "It's my turn, Papa!" Then he pushed the stool away and played. His legs were too short for him to play the organ while seated, so he worked the foot pedals while standing up! The little boy played as though he'd been practicing for months.

Paris and Versailles

The back wheel fixed, the Mozarts resumed their trip. Slowly they passed through Germany, giving concerts in different towns along the way. Finally, on November 18, 1763, they arrived in Paris. The family felt a little lost at first. Paris was a fun-loving, sophisticated city. It was different from any city the Mozarts had ever visited. The children gave several small concerts. Though they were the talk of the town, no important invitations to perform were received. After a month, Leopold decided to go to the nearby town of Versailles, where the king of France had his court.

On New Year's Day, 1764, they received a summons from King Louis XV. The family was to attend a public court dinner. This was a great honor for the Mozarts. The French royalty didn't dine in public very often, except for great festivals. Even then, only important people would be invited. And no one but the royal family would actually be seated at a table.

The Mozarts arrived late. To the family's surprise, the Swiss Guards escorted them through the crowded hall to a spot right behind the king and queen. The eight-year-old Mozart was allowed to stand beside the queen the entire time! Not afraid at all, he chatted with her and kissed her hands. Before long she was laughing and feeding him the best treats from the royal table.

The French noblemen who were there saw how importantly the Mozarts were treated. Invitations to perform soon came pouring in. Besides playing concerts, the family was able to meet many noted musicians. They also met actors, singers, and dancers.

When they returned to Paris a short time later, they found that now there was a lot more interest in the talented Mozart children. The children soon gave a concert that was a big success. People gave them a lot of money, which made Leopold very happy. Often, instead of money, people would give them gifts. These included watches, clothes, and bits of fine lace. The gifts were nice, but they didn't put food on the table or pay for traveling expenses, as Leopold often grumbled.

London

Successful as they were in Paris, there were still no likely patrons in sight. The Mozarts decided to go London, England. Leopold hired a boat to take them across the English Channel. None of them had ever seen the sea before. By the time they arrived at the port of Dover, they were all seasick. "Mama, the ground is moving!" Mozart cried when they finally set foot on land.

Their discomfort soon turned to excitement. Crossing the old London Bridge in a coach, they watched the Thames River beneath them. It was packed with all sorts of ships and boats. Before them, the spires of London's buildings rose majestically in the air. It was April 23, 1764.

London was a rich city. Unlike Paris, it wasn't just the nobility who had a lot of money. Merchants and traders were wealthy, too, and were willing to pay for concerts. This fact served the Mozarts well. In the 15 months they were in London, they made more money than in any other city.

Also contributing to their success was the fact that London was a music-loving city. The king and queen were great supporters of the arts. After being in London only five days, the Mozarts were given a royal summons to perform for the court.

Queen Charlotte and King George III—the same king the Americans would fight in the Revolution—gave the family a very warm welcome. Dressed in fancy new English clothes, the children performed well. Mozart played Bach and Handel on sight, without having practiced at all. He also accompanied Queen Charlotte as she sang an aria.

The best part, though, was being introduced to the court composer, Johann Christian Bach. He was the son of the great composer, Johann Sebastian Bach. The court composer was very interested in Mozart's compositions. Unlike many other court musicians, Bach wasn't a bit put off that Mozart was still a young child. The two musicians spent a lot of time together. Often they'd improvise for the king and queen on the same clavier—with Mozart sitting on Bach's lap!

About two months after they'd arrived in London, the Mozart family put on a big concert. For part of it, Mozart accompanied Italian singers as they performed arias he had written himself. To Leopold's great joy, the concert brought in a great deal of money.

In those days, illness was never far away. This time it was Leopold who got sick. The family rented a little house in Chelsea for the summer, hoping that the country air would help Leopold recover. The children were told to be very quiet.

They couldn't even play their instruments.

Although Mozart missed practicing his music, he loved the seven weeks the family spent in the country. Most of his time was spent composing. He even wrote his first symphony! Called Symphony in E Flat Major, it was dedicated to Mozart's good friend, court composer Johann Christian Bach. "He is by far the nicest man I've ever met," the young Mozart announced fondly as he worked on the difficult piece.

Mozart wrote many other pieces that summer as well. Today these are known as the "Chelsea Notebook." Since leaving Salzburg, Mozart had developed his talents a great deal. Being around other gifted musicians had taught him a lot.

How Can a Child Play So Well?

When Leopold got well, the family returned to London. But now they had a new problem to face. Jealous musicians had been spreading a rumor about Mozart. They claimed that Mozart was really much older than he looked. "No young child could possibly play so well!" they exclaimed.

A well-known lawyer became curious about the child musician. After sending for Mozart's birth certificate, he spent many hours with the boy, observing and testing him. The "tests" included playing very difficult pieces on sight, as well as improvising on certain themes. Far from being scared, Mozart did as the lawyer requested. "Do you have anything else for me to play?" he asked eagerly. Music was music, after all.

The lawyer was amazed at Mozart's skills. But even though Mozart could play better than most adults, he still acted like the young boy he was. One day, as he was playing for the lawyer, Mozart's favorite cat came into the room. "Here, kitty, kitty!" Mozart called out in his high, piping voice. He dashed away from the clavier and played with his pet for a while. Neither Leopold nor the lawyer could get him to come back—at least, not until the ruffled cat had run out of the room.

This was not the only example of Mozart's child-like actions. As the lawyer later wrote, "He would also sometimes run about the room with a stick between his legs, by way of a horse."

At last the lawyer obtained the record of Mozart's birth from the register at Salzburg. Then Londoners found out that the family had been telling the truth all along.

Holland

After 15 months in London, the children received fewer and fewer invitations to perform. Their income started to drop. Finally, Leopold told his family, "I think it's time we go on to Holland." Mozart was sorry to leave. He especially hated saying good-bye to Johann Christian Bach. He hoped that when he was older, he could come back to London. Unfortunately, he never did.

As soon as they arrived in Holland, illness struck once more. Nannerl came down with typhus. She became delirious, calling out strange things in all the languages she had learned— German, French, Italian, and English. In spite of their worry, the family couldn't help but laugh at the funny things she said.

Just as Nannerl started getting better, her brother caught the same disease. It hit Mozart even harder. Lying in his bed, the feverish Mozart made the gestures of an orchestra conductor. For a long time he couldn't even talk. Then one day he weakly told his mother, "I want to go to the keyboard, Mama." The family sighed in relief. Mozart was getting well!

After they recovered, the children gave some well-received concerts at the Dutch court. Then, after a brief stay in Paris, they started for home. Whenever possible, they gave performances in different cities along the way. On the very last day of November 1776, they arrived back in Salzburg.

Trouble in the Hometown

Leopold was worried. They'd been gone for more than three years—much longer than he'd expected. He was afraid that he'd lost his position with the court in Salzburg. Nervously, he went to see the Archbishop. Then he found out that he hadn't been dismissed after all. His salary had been stopped, however, and he was told that from then on he would only be paid for the time he spent in Salzburg.

This didn't deter Mozart's father. Busily, Leopold set about planning the next steps of Mozart's career. He still thought that his talented son would bring the family fame and riches.

In the meantime, both Nannerl and Mozart worked very hard. Besides practicing their music, they kept up with their other studies as well. Mozart's favorite was math. When he first got the hang of it, he even put his music aside for a little while. He ran all about the house, scribbling numbers with chalk wherever he could. Anna Maria patiently cleaned up after him. Her little Wolferl was so funny that she couldn't stay mad at him for long.

But it wasn't always pleasant to be back in their hometown. The townspeople were jealous of Mozart and often talked down to him. Mozart was a good-natured child, but this made him very angry. To make matters worse, another rumor was making the rounds. People thought that Mozart was getting help with his composing. They found it hard to believe that anyone so young could write such good music.

Even the archbishop of Salzburg challenged him. He had Mozart stay in the palace for a week, seeing nobody but the servants who brought him his meals. During the week Mozart wrote a very fine—and very long—oratorio. At last, the rumors stopped.

3 CHAPTER | SUCCESS AND DEFEAT

*"God probably has something
else in mind for us."*

—Leopold on Mozart's failure
to obtain a court position

On the Road Again

When Mozart was 11 years old, the family went to Vienna for a short visit. The empress' daughter was getting married. There would be festivities of all kinds, and music would be needed. Leopold hoped to find work for the children. Sadly, the empress' daughter caught smallpox and died before the wedding. No vaccinations existed then. People lived under the threat of epidemics. Scared, Leopold brought his family back home as quickly as he could. Mozart came down with the disease anyway. It was only a mild case, however, and he soon recovered.

The following January, Leopold and Mozart returned to Vienna, where they would stay for an entire year. At the request of Emperor Joseph II, Mozart wrote his first opera. It was called *La Finta Semplice* (The Simple Pretense). But the court musicians were angry at the idea of a child in the conductor's spot. They made sure that the actors and musicians wouldn't cooperate. The opera was never performed.

Mozart was very disappointed, but he went on composing. One of his new pieces was a mass that was performed in the emperor's private chapel.

One day, for the fun of it, Leopold made a list of all of his son's compositions. By that time, Mozart had written more than 80 pieces! Many of them are still performed today.

Returning to Salzburg in January 1769, the Mozarts had a surprise. The archbishop of Salzburg had heard about the opera Mozart had written for the emperor. He arranged for Mozart's opera to be performed. Even the jealous people of Salzburg knew the opera was a success. This victory helped make up for some of the disappointments in Vienna.

Italy

Not quite a year later, Leopold and Wolfgang left on a trip to Italy. At that time, Italy was not an independent country. Parts of it were ruled by France, Spain, and Austria. The trip started out well. As Mozart wrote to his mother, "It is so much fun on this trip! The carriage is so warm. And our coachman drives fast whenever he can!"

All through their long journey, the only way to keep in touch with Anna Maria and Nannerl was through letters. No other means of long-distance communication existed at that time. Because paper was handmade and costly, people covered every inch with tiny writing. Envelopes hadn't been invented yet, so people just folded or rolled up the paper. And all that was required for an address was a name and a city. That was because very few people could read or write—and those who could were well known within their city.

Verona was Leopold's and Mozart's first major stop. The carnival season was taking place, which made it even more exciting. Here Mozart heard his first Italian opera in its native land. To his delight, everyone in the audience had to wear a mask! Mozart also gave a concert at the Accademia Filarmonica. A rich man in the audience was so impressed that he hired an artist to paint a portrait of the boy. And when Mozart was practicing the organ one day in a church, a huge crowd formed outside the doors. Mozart and his father had to sneak out through the attached monastery. They were afraid of being mobbed!

From Verona the two musicians went to Mantura, Milan, Bologna, and Florence. Mozart especially liked Milan. He and Leopold went to the opera as often as they could, and to masked balls afterwards. In his letters to Nannerl, Mozart described all the things they were doing. He was often very funny—and sometimes very rude. In one letter he told about an opera they'd seen. "The lead singer is not so bad, but is rather ancient and ugly as sin. The second singer looks like a fish!" he wrote.

Finally, Leopold and Mozart arrived in Rome. In the Vatican, they visited Michelangelo's Sistine Chapel. There, they heard *Miserere*, a difficult choral work by Allegri. As soon as Mozart got back to his room, he grabbed a pen and paper. He had soon written down the entire piece from memory!

This was a very remarkable thing to do. It was also very brave, for it was against church law to make a copy of the Papal Choir's music. But when people learned about Mozart's feat, no one complained about that. Instead, many concerts were arranged as word spread about the amazing thing Mozart had done. People wanted to see this incredible boy for themselves.

Next came a trip to Naples. The journey was thought to be very dangerous. Rumor had it that gangs of highway bandits lurked along the road. "Papa, do you think we're going to be robbed?" Mozart asked as they bounced down the road in their carriage. Leopold just frowned worriedly and shrugged his shoulders. Luckily, they made the trip unharmed.

They spent a happy month in Naples and then came back to Rome. There, Mozart received a great honor. On June 26, 1770, Pope Clement IX named Mozart a Knight of the Order of the Golden Spur. He gave Mozart a gold cross on a red ribbon in honor of his musical abilities. Mozart was only the second musician to get such an award.

The young composer even got to see the pope in person. Although that was a big thrill, Mozart never took the knighthood itself too seriously. About the only time he ever brought it up was when he wanted to tease Nannerl.

After their stay in Rome, Leopold and Mozart went to Bologna. From there they had to go back to Milan, where Mozart had been commissioned to write an opera. *Mitridate, Rè di Ponto* (Mithridatus, King of Pontus) was performed the day after Christmas. Mozart himself conducted it. The people of Milan liked the opera so much that 20 performances were given. Each time, the audience would call out "Long live the maestro!"

The Mozarts' carriage rolled back into Salzburg at the end of March 1771. At first, Anna and Nannerl could hardly recognize Mozart. "Is this really our little Wolferl?" they teased. He had done a lot of growing while he'd been away, and most of his clothes were too small. His voice had changed, too. The days of being a child wonder were gone. Mozart was now 15 years old.

Back in Salzburg, Mozart was as busy as ever. The Milan court had commissioned him to compose music for a royal wedding that fall. They also wanted him to write another opera for the carnival season. For five months Mozart worked on the music. He also spent as much time with his mother and sister as he possibly could. Then he and Leopold left once more for Milan.

The opera was a success. In fact, the court was so pleased with him that besides paying him the normal fee, they gave him a gold watch set with diamonds. But despite all the praise and gifts, what Leopold and Mozart wanted most—a permanent court appointment—was not offered. A little discouraged, father and son returned to Salzburg.

A New Archbishop

In the spring of 1772, the Archbishop of Salzburg died. This event had a big effect on the Mozarts, as well as on other musicians. The new archbishop, Count von Colloredo, was a stern, unpleasant man. He especially disliked Leopold and his talented son. He felt they thought too much of themselves. Besides that, 16-year-old Mozart was short, and short people had always annoyed the Count.

But Count von Colloredo was no fool. He knew that Mozart was an important composer. Keeping Mozart in Salzburg would make the court—and the count—look good in the eyes of others. Grudgingly he gave Mozart a position as a court musician, though Mozart was paid very little.

Leopold was allowed to keep his job, but he, too, suffered under the new archbishop's reign. When a vacancy came up for the position of head Kappellmeister, Leopold was passed over. This made the family very upset, for Leopold had been the obvious choice for the job. Living in Salzburg had become a real trial.

Still, Mozart was hopeful. Another opera had been commissioned for the Milan carnival season. With great excitement, Leopold and Wolfgang went to Milan for the premiere. But the people of Milan didn't really like *Luccio Silla*. Mozart had done some experimenting with the music, and the opera was too different from what people were used to. The Milan court never commissioned another one after that. "God probably has something else in mind for us," Leopold sighed as he and Mozart returned to Salzburg.

In 1775, Mozart got another chance. The 18-year-old musician was asked to compose a new opera for the carnival season in Munich. Leopold and Mozart went to Munich in December to finish the preparations. While he was working on the opera, Mozart suffered from a terrible toothache. But he was so happy to be working on an opera again—and to be away from Salzburg—that he ignored it as best he could. Despite his pain, he was cheerful and full of jokes.

Mozart couldn't get away from his problems for long, however. Count von Colloredo happened to be in Munich at the same time. The count made a point of not attending the premiere of *La Finta Giardiniera* (The Disguised Gardner's Girl). But the opera was very successful. Everywhere he went, he heard people sing Mozart's praises. Count von Colloredo just shrugged his shoulders. After that, he was even more unpleasant to the Mozarts.

For the next two years, Mozart and Leopold stayed in Salzburg. They lived quietly and tried not to anger the archbishop. Working hard at their composing, they found comfort in their music. Then matters came to a head.

Anxiously, Leopold approached his employer to ask for another leave. He wanted to travel with his son again. Although the request was not out of line for musicians in those days, the archbishop refused to grant the leave. Angrily he declared that Mozart knew nothing. "He ought to go to a conservatory in Naples to learn something about music!" the archbishop shouted.

Before anyone could stop him, Mozart handed in his resignation. He didn't need to put up with this! Leopold worried for days that he himself would be fired. Then what would the family do? As it turned out, Count von Colloredo allowed him keep his job. Leopold was very relieved. Still, his position would never again bring much happiness to him.

Mozart was now 21 years old. He was full of life, and very confident of his talents. He wanted to travel and look for a court position on his own. Leopold wouldn't hear of it. He knew his son.

Mozart, left to himself, would fritter away any money he earned. And what if he got caught up with some foolish friends? Or started running after women? No, that could not be allowed to happen!

Leopold was right in worrying about his son. But it wasn't all Mozart's fault. All of his life, Leopold had been making the decisions. Mozart was now an adult, but he had never had a chance to stand on his own.

In time, Leopold changed his mind. Mozart could travel, but his mother would have to go along, Leopold decided. She might not be able to arrange the introductions, but at least she could keep an eye on Mozart. Anna Maria didn't want to go. She hated to leave her pleasant home. But she knew that there was no other way. After all, how much trouble could a young man get into with his mother right there?

A statue of Mozart stands in his hometown of Salzburg, Austria.

Many of the buildings from Mozart's day still stand in Salzburg. Mozart's father, Leopold, was the Vice-Kappellmeister (concert master) for the Salzburg court.

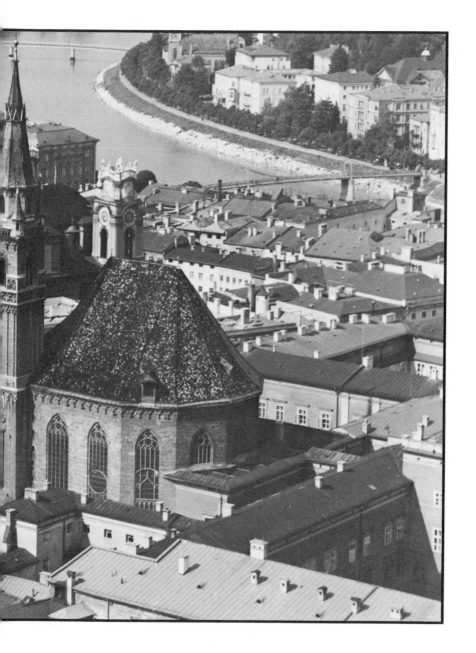

Mozart's Geburtshaus (birthplace) is a much-visited site in Salzburg.

Mozart took his music very seriously, but he was also a fun-loving man. His outgoing nature won him many friends—and a few jealous enemies he referred to as "snakes in the grass."

Music was always very important in the Mozart house-hold. The illustration above shows Mozart and his sister, Nannerl, playing a duet while Leopold looks on.

Leopold Mozart—and later his famous son—often passed by this fountain in the Salzburg court. The Mozarts lived in a tall, narrow building nearby.

Although people were amazed at Mozart's talent, he was 31 before he received a permanent court position—and a poorly paid one at that.

*At the age of 17, Ludwig van Beethoven traveled to Vienna
in hopes of studying with Mozart. This illustration shows
Beethoven at the piano, as Mozart and his friends look on.*

Tourists to both Vienna and Salzburg make it a point to visit the areas associated with Mozart's life. This picture shows the Mirabell Garden in Salzburg.

Music surrounded Mozart even in his last days. He is shown here with his wife, Constanze, and their musician friends.

4 CHAPTER | MOZART ON HIS OWN

"*I am just beginning to live.*"

—Mozart declaring his
independence from his father

A Dark-Eyed Beauty

In September 1777, Anna Maria and Mozart set off for Munich. "Write often!" Nannerl begged. She and Leopold were going to miss the other half of their family.

As soon as they arrived in Munich, Mozart went to see the elector of Bavaria. He told the elector about his accomplishments. Then he asked for a position with the court. "I'm sorry, my dear boy," the elector told him. "There is no vacancy." With that he swept out of the room. Mozart was left bowing.

From there, Mozart and his mother went to Augsburg, where they stayed with some cousins. They soon found that no position was open there, either, so they headed for Mannheim.

Mannheim was famous throughout Europe for its music. Musicians from that area stressed feeling and emotion in their music. They made use of soft tones as well as very loud ones. They also introduced opera sung in German, rather than in

Italian. Mozart hoped to learn from the Mannheim musicians while he looked for a position.

Mozart soon made many friends. He spent his days composing, giving lessons and concerts, and dining out with his new companions. Then, just after his 22nd birthday, Mozart fell in love.

Among his friends in Mannheim was a man named Fridolin Weber. Weber was poor, with a large family of daughters to support. He was a music copyist, as well as an opera singer for the court. Mozart hadn't been friends with him long before he started noticing Weber's daughter, Aloysia. At 15 she was already a very good singer. Besides that, she was pretty—with black curly hair and dark eyes.

One afternoon Mozart gathered up his courage. He asked Aloysia to sing for him. "Here? Today?" she asked shyly. "Why not? The clavier's right here for me to accompany you," Mozart bravely replied. At last Aloysia agreed. Mozart was delighted. From then on, he spent a lot of time composing pieces for Aloysia to sing.

Mozart was so happy! He couldn't help but drop

hints of his first love in letters to his father. This horrified Leopold. The last thing Mozart needed right now was a wife! And she wasn't even from a rich family! Leopold started writing his son long, angry letters. He ordered Mozart to go to Paris at once. Mozart just kept putting it off. "We'll go in the springtime," he wrote. Then he cleverly added, "Traveling won't be so hard on Mama when the weather is nicer."

Soon another letter arrived. In this one, Leopold wrote in great detail about the sacrifices he had made so his son could travel. He was deeply in debt. He was forced to dress in old clothes. He even had to eat cheap food. The letter really got to Mozart. He hated being told what to do, but he hated feeling guilty even more! Before long he wrote to Leopold, "About Paris. We shall leave in a week."

Saying good-bye to the Weber family—especially Aloysia—was difficult. Even the younger daughters cried to see him leave. But Mozart didn't feel he had a choice. At the end of March 1778, he and his mother arrived in Paris.

Tragedy
in Paris

The queen of France was now Marie Antoinette. She was the young princess who had helped Mozart off the floor many years ago in Vienna. Hoping that she would remember him, Mozart went to see her. Queen Marie Antoinette showed very little interest in him, however. There were so many musicians around. To her, Mozart was just part of the crowd.

The noblemen were cold and unfriendly as well. Mozart was unhappy and composed very little. He daydreamed about Aloysia, and wrote long letters to her and the rest of the Weber family. Aloysia never answered, but that didn't stop Mozart from thinking about her.

Anna Maria wasn't enjoying the stay in Paris any more than Mozart was. She had no friends. Because they had very little money, she seldom got to go out. They lived in a small apartment with very little sunlight, where she spent most of her time alone. The hallways were too narrow to bring in the clavier. This meant that Mozart had to do his composing elsewhere. In a sad letter to her husband, Anna Maria wrote, "I do not see Wolferl all day and will soon forget completely how to talk."

Then Anna Maria became ill. All the traveling, all the moving from place to place had been too exhausting for her. At first she tried to hide her illness from Mozart. She didn't want to worry him. But after a while she couldn't hide it any longer. Despite suffering from chills, a high fever, and headaches, she refused to see a doctor. "I will have no French poisoner," she said in as firm a voice as she could.

Finally, Mozart found a German doctor who lived in Paris. The doctor gave her his best cure—rhubarb powder in wine—but it didn't help. Anna Maria died on July 3, 1778.

Mozart was heartbroken. How could he tell his father and sister this terrible news? Because they already knew she was ill, Mozart wrote them a letter saying she had taken a turn for the worse. Then he wrote another letter, with the real story, to a family friend in Salzburg. He asked this friend to break the news gently to his father and sister.

Grieving for his mother, Mozart then wrote Leopold that he would be returning to Salzburg. But he couldn't bring himself to go directly home. Instead, he slowly traveled through Germany. Eventually he arrived at Munich, where the Webers were now living.

Dashed Dreams

Mozart went to visit the Weber family on Christmas Day. The fortune of the Webers had changed since he had seen them last. Aloysia was now earning a large salary as an opera singer. When Mozart arrived at the Weber home, a party was going on. Musicians and singers of all sorts were milling about. At the center of it all was Aloysia. She was taller and more sophisticated than Mozart remembered. To his eyes, she was more beautiful than ever.

Mozart made his way through the crowd. Trembling, he bowed and kissed her hand. But Aloysia just looked at him coldly. Turning to the fellow next to her, she made a sarcastic comment about Mozart's appearance. All the people standing nearby laughed.

His heart pounding, Mozart forced himself to smile. He clicked his heels together and made a sweeping bow. Then, with all eyes on him, he walked over to the clavier. Taking a deep breath, he started to sing a funny little song everyone knew. It was the only way he could hide what he was feeling.

For a whole year, Mozart had been living with the dream of someday sharing his future with Aloysia. Now, in one moment, his hopes were shattered. He became a little less trusting after this experience, but he managed to maintain his friendship with the Webers. Eventually, he and Aloysia even became friends again—though they were never very close.

Mozart had now run out of excuses. He went back to Salzburg as he had promised. Tearfully, Leopold and Nannerl welcomed him home. It was hard to see him without Anna Maria.

Mozart's travels had been a failure. He hadn't made very much money, and he had not found a position. The family was now deeper in debt than ever before. Gritting his teeth, Mozart went to the Count von Colloredo and asked for his old job back. He'd always hated pretending to like the nobility, and this was the worst yet! The count gave him the job, but didn't make things any easier for Mozart. "The bright young man had to come back home!" he gloated.

More problems were ahead. Mozart was nearly 24 years old, and he resented his father for always treating him like a child. True, Leopold was very encouraging when it came to music. But when it came to other things, nothing Mozart did was ever right. Leopold knew his son was a genius. Still, he seemed to expect Mozart to act like an ordinary person—and a boring one at that. There was a lot of conflict between father and son.

Money worries were always in the back of their minds. Impressed with Mozart's music, the nobility often gave Mozart presents instead of the money the family needed. Pawning the gifts was out of the question—for the time being, at least. It would seem too tacky. At one point, Mozart had five costly watches. He told his father, "I'm seriously thinking about wearing one watch on each leg of my trousers when I visit some great lord, so it will not occur to him to give me another one!"

Mozart also complained about the dull Salzburg audiences. "It seems like the audience is made of nothing but tables and chairs," he once said in frustration. It was a dismal period in his life. Surprisingly, though, the compositions written during this phase didn't reflect his depressed state of mind. The music, as always, was an outlet and a joy.

Free at Last

Before long, Mozart got the break he'd been hoping for. The Munich court asked him to write another opera. It would be performed during the carnival season of 1781. Muttering all the while, Count von Colloredo granted him a six-week leave of absence. Mozart went to Munich in high spirits. *Idomeneo* was performed at the end of January. The opera was a big success.

Mozart was having such a good time with his friends in Munich that he didn't want to go home. Pretty soon, he had put Salzburg out of his mind completely. His six-week leave stretched to four months. Finally, the count lost patience. He ordered Mozart to join him in Vienna, where he'd be staying for a while. Meekly, Mozart did as he was told. At least he wouldn't have to go back to Salzburg yet. He hoped he could be on his own a little while longer.

But in Vienna, Count von Colloredo treated him like a lowly servant. Mozart was forced to live in the servants' quarters, and take his meals with them as well. But that was not all. For two months Mozart could appear only in musicales sponsored by the count. He couldn't take on any new commissions. Mozart's letters to Leopold were filled with complaints. "His vanity is tickled by possessing my person—but what use is all this to me? One cannot live on it! And I assure you he acts as a screen to keep me from the notice of others!"

Then the Archbishop rudely ordered all his musicians back to Salzburg. Mozart refused to go, which resulted in several noisy quarrels. "Scoundrel!" the count shouted at Mozart. "Miserable wretch!" Shaking with rage, Mozart once again handed in his resignation. This time it was final. Never again would he be employed in the count's service.

Of course, Leopold was very upset by Mozart's rashness. What if he couldn't find a position elsewhere? How would he live? But Mozart, feeling free and sure of himself, dismissed Leopold's fears.

Soon he gave his overprotective father something else to worry about.

A New Commitment

The Weber family was now living in Vienna. The family had undergone some changes, however. Fridolin, the father, had died shortly after the move. Aloysia had married an actor. To make ends meet, Mrs. Weber was renting out rooms to lodgers. Mozart wasted no time moving in.

Mrs. Weber was a scheming woman. She wanted Mozart to marry one of her other daughters. True, he was poor. But his chances of making it big were as good as those of any other musician. Mrs. Weber and her daughters did all they could to make Mozart feel at home. They fixed his clothes. They held supper for him when he was late, and took care of his every need. Naturally, Mozart loved all the attention!

Mrs. Weber's plan seemed to be working. Mozart was spending more and more time with Constanze, who was now 18. Like her sister Aloysia, Constanze had curly black hair and dark eyes. She wasn't quite as pretty as her sister, and she had little musical talent. But "Stanze," as Mozart fondly called her, was smart and easy to be with. "She has the kindest heart in the world," he said.

Before long, Leopold heard rumors from his musician friends that Mozart was falling in love with Constanze. He was worried sick. He didn't trust the Webers one bit, and saw through all the scheming. Mozart tried to reassure his father that he wasn't thinking of getting married. To prove it, he even moved out of the Webers' house. Probably no one was very convinced, though—least of all Mozart himself. It wasn't long afterwards that Mozart and Constanze became engaged.

This was a very enjoyable time for Mozart. He was giving music lessons, and being paid very well to do it. He'd published six new violin sonatas. Crowds of people were coming to his concerts. He'd even written another opera, *Il Seraglio, Die Entführung* (The Abduction from the Seraglio).

Seraglio was the first comic opera sung in German. It was also the first one to have real dramatic characters. Until then, opera parts just showed off the singers' voices. Little acting ability was needed. The new opera was a big hit. Mozart had high hopes that a permanent position would soon be his.

The only thing that marred this period was his father's refusal to give him permission to marry. Leopold's permission wasn't required, of course, but 26-year-old Mozart wanted it anyway. Angry letters went back and forth. Finally Mozart had had enough. He married Constanze Weber on August 4, 1782, in St. Stephen's Cathedral in Vienna. Describing the ceremony the next day in a letter to his father, Mozart wrote: "All present, even the priest, were deeply touched and all wept to see how much our hearts were moved."

Leopold, though, didn't take the news well. As he had grown older, he had become very bitter about all the disappointments that had come his way. Leopold told Mozart that he was now completely on his own. But he didn't say that he wouldn't come to visit, or that Mozart should stop writing to him.

The break between father and son had finally happened. From now on, Mozart would make his own decisions, in both personal and business matters. He would take the consequences, come what may. This didn't scare Mozart. "I am just beginning to live," he said.

5
CHAPTER

A
HOME
IN VIENNA

*"This young man will make a noise
in the world someday."*

**—Mozart upon meeting
Ludwig van Beethoven**

A Full Life

Life in the Mozart household was far from ordinary. Although Constanze tried, she was never a very good housekeeper. And the way Mozart handled money bothered her. Being married to an unpredictable genius must have been difficult. But, treating each other like playmates, they enjoyed each other's company. When they had to be apart, they missed each other terribly.

Mozart and Constanze liked being around other people. They had a lot of friends in Vienna, and went to balls and parties whenever they possibly could. The first winter they were married, they even gave a ball themselves. This was a great luxury, because they couldn't really afford it. The ball lasted from 6 o'clock in the evening to 7 o'clock the following morning. Everyone had a lot of fun.

In June 1783, the Mozarts' first child, a son, was born. Soon afterwards, they decided to visit Leopold and Nannerl in Salzburg. They left the baby with foster parents in Vienna, which was the custom in those days. In Salzburg, the visit went as well as they could have hoped. Leopold still didn't accept Constanze. But she did her best to be charming and agreeable to her father-in-law. For his part, Leopold did his best to hold back any harsh comments.

Still, Mozart and Constanze were very relieved when the visit was over. Salzburg, with all its memories of disappointment, was as unbearable to Mozart as it had ever been. He was glad they lived in Vienna.

They did not have a pleasant homecoming, however. While they had been gone, their baby had gotten sick and died. Wolfgang and Constanze were very upset, but they soon got over their grief. People at that time were accustomed to babies dying. They didn't have the medical knowledge to provide good care. Eventually, Mozart and Constanze had six babies. Only two of them lived.

Throwing himself into his work, Mozart kept up his busy pace. The constant rounds of lessons, composing, concerts, and parties was exhausting. No one was surprised when, in the spring of 1784, he became ill.

Every year of Mozart's life had been marked by some illness or another. He'd lived a very intense life since the age of six, when he first started touring. All the traveling in drafty coaches, all the years spent in poorly heated apartments had seriously affected his health. And in those days, doctors' prescriptions were often wrong. Sometimes the treatment killed patients even before the illness did! It's a wonder that Mozart lived as long as he did.

Mozart spent the whole summer recovering. His spirits were boosted when Constanze gave birth to another son. They named him Karl.

In the meantime, Mozart's sister Nannerl had married. She was over 30, and for years Leopold had fussed and fretted about his daughter being "on the shelf." Without Nannerl living with him, however, Leopold became very lonely. He decided to pay Constanze and Mozart a visit.

By this time Mozart had recovered from his illness. He rushed Leopold about, taking him from concert to concert. Everywhere they went, people were overflowing with praise for Mozart. Leopold finally put to rest his idea that his son wasn't living up to his musical genius. He even half-heartedly accepted Constanze and their style of living. Wanting Leopold's approval, Mozart and his wife had been very careful about not seeming too extravagant.

But Leopold was now an old man. He couldn't keep up the frantic pace. And the house was so noisy! Besides a young baby and constant music, there was a very lively dog named Guckel. They also had an ever-chirping bird named Starl. The bird could even whistle the theme from one of Mozart's piano concerts! Mozart was delighted with this trick. For Leopold, though, it was just too much. After a while he decided to go back home. Mozart never saw Salzburg or his father again.

A Bold New Opera

During the spring and summer of 1785, Mozart worked on another opera called *The Marriage of Figaro*. Writing the libretto, or text, of the opera was Lorenzo da Ponte. Da Ponte was the court poet in Vienna. He liked Mozart's witty talk, and the two men quickly became good friends.

Figaro told the story of a poor writer who, in order to make a living, was forced to become the servant of a haughty, rich Spaniard. In the story, it was the nobleman—not his servant—who was made to look like a fool.

This expressed some bold ideas that were very much in keeping with the times. People were starting to talk about the rights of the individual. They questioned the idea that some people were better than others simply because they happened to be born into an aristocratic family. A person's talent and ability, not heritage, should be what counted.

Naturally, Mozart identified with this new line of thinking. He'd been struggling with an unfair system all of his life. His new opera allowed him to express, through music, some of his views.

Figaro had its share of problems, however. The jealous court musicians, as usual, tried to bring Mozart down a notch or two. Mozart called them "snakes in the grass." These musicians tried to prevent the opera from being performed. When that didn't work, they tried to convince the singers to bungle their parts. Only an order from the emperor got the singers to do their best. *Figaro* was a success—but only for a short while. The Viennese people soon forgot about it.

Not everyone was so quick to dismiss Mozart. In the city of Prague, (now the capital of Czechoslovakia), Mozart was regarded as a true genius. Ever since Mozart's opera, *Seraglio*, had been performed there three years earlier, the people of Prague had considered Mozart the greatest musician of all.

Figaro was performed in Prague in December 1786. The theater was packed for all the performances. After the final curtain, people even threw poems onto the stage, praising the work. When he heard about his latest success, Mozart visited the city the next month. The people of Prague liked Mozart so much that they commissioned him to write another opera. It was wonderful to be appreciated for a change!

Tragedy and Triumph

Back in Vienna, life soon became difficult again. Constanze was sick, and often had to go to a health resort under doctors' orders. This was very expensive. Money problems were always on Mozart's mind. Besides that, he really missed Constanze whenever she was gone.

One day, as he was working on the new Prague opera, there was a knock on the door. Standing in the doorway was a stocky teenage boy, asking for the honor of taking piano lessons from Mozart. At first Mozart was annoyed. No doubt the boy was talentless, like so many of the others coming to his door. But as he listened to the boy play, he was amazed. "This young man will make a noise in the world someday," he announced. The boy's name was Ludwig van Beethoven.

Mozart didn't have much time for his new pupil, however. The young Beethoven patiently waited for the day when Mozart would become his instructor. Then, after just two weeks, Beethoven had to leave town. His mother was very ill, and he had to go back home to Bonn, Germany, to take care of her.

Illness was everywhere, it seemed. Leopold died on May 28, 1787. Mozart himself was too sick to travel to Salzburg for the funeral. It was a long, sorrow-filled summer for the Mozart family.

As soon as he recovered from his illness, Mozart turned to his music in relief. He and Lorenzo da Ponte worked on the new Prague opera, *Don Giovanni*. It was a story about a man who fell in love with every pretty woman he met. At the end of October, Mozart went to Prague to finish the music for the opera. He took Constanze with him.

Two days before the premiere, Mozart still hadn't written the overture, or opening piece, for the opera. His friends were frantic about it. Mozart just laughed. As with all of his composing, the overture was already finished in his head. All that remained was writing it down on paper.

The night before the premiere, Mozart went to a big party held for the people involved with the show. Ignoring all the remarks about the unfinished overture, he set about having a good time. Finally, around midnight, he disappeared. Constanze was missing too—as was a huge jug of rum punch! As Mozart worked, Constanze kept him awake by telling him fairy tales. By 7 o'clock the next morning, the overture was done.

The premiere of *Don Giovanni* went off without a hitch—even though the musicians hadn't had a chance to practice the overture once. The citizens of Prague went crazy for Mozart and his music once again. "Stay here with us a little while longer!" they begged. Tempting as it was, Mozart went back home to Vienna. He knew that if he stayed, he would soon be taken for granted. That's what had always happened in the past, and he didn't want to go through that again.

An Appointment At Last

Mozart went back to Vienna for another reason as well. The famous court composer, Christoph Gluck, had died on November 15. Gluck's position was now open. How Mozart hoped to finally get an appointment to the court! He knew that there were a lot of other musicians in the city angling for the post. Most of them were his enemies. But at last the decision was announced. Wolfgang Amadeus Mozart was the new Imperial and Royal Court Composer.

Unfortunately, the good news didn't change his life all that much. His salary was small, less than half of what Gluck had received. It hardly covered the rent. Still, it was regular employment. At 31, Mozart finally got the post his father had spent his life trying to obtain for his son. If Leopold had lived six months longer, he would have been very proud.

The following spring, *Don Giovanni* was performed for the first time in Vienna. It didn't go over as well as it had in Prague. The people didn't like it at first, but they spent a lot of time discussing it. A few dedicated Mozart fans insisted on more performances. Eventually, the people of Vienna decided that it was one of the best operas ever written. That didn't happen soon enough to help Mozart, however.

Karl, the Mozarts now had a six-month-old daughter named Theresa. Just 10 days after they moved to their new home, the baby girl died.

It was during this unhappy time that Mozart wrote three of his greatest symphonies, one right after another. He finished them in just six weeks. They were called Symphony in E Flat Major, Symphony in G Minor, and the *Jupiter* Symphony. Many people today feel that these three symphonies were the greatest of all Mozart's achievements.

Living in the country seemed to work out well when it came to Mozart's composing, but there were drawbacks, too. His piano students weren't able to get to the country house very easily. Soon the family moved back to the city. By this time, moving was very easy. Most of their furniture had been pawned!

A dark phase was beginning. Fewer and fewer people attended Mozart's concerts. This depressed him so much that he composed very little. At 33, he was poorer than ever before. He had to borrow money from friends just to keep going.

was poorer than ever before. He had to borrow money from friends just to keep going.

Another Journey

In the spring of 1789, Mozart got another chance to get away from Vienna for a while. A nobleman friend suggested that Mozart come with him to Berlin. On the way, they'd stop at Prague, Leipzig, and Dresden. Mozart accepted the invitation eagerly.

While they were at Leipzig, Mozart was able to play the church organ that had been used by the great Johann Sebastian Bach. Bach was the father of his childhood friend, the court composer in London. Mozart had always been an admirer of Bach's work. Playing the organ was a very moving experience for him.

In Berlin, Mozart was delighted to find that his opera, *Il Seraglio*, was being performed. At first he crept into the back of the theater to listen. Then he started to get excited by the music. Without being aware of it, he slowly edged his way to the front, humming to himself as he walked.

The audience snickered at this small, strange man. Mozart was so absorbed in the music that he didn't even notice. When the second violinist played a wrong note, Mozart lost all control. "Damn it all!" he shouted. "**Will** you play D!" The people recognized him then. Whispers of "Mozart is here!" passed through the crowd.

Mozart arrived home in Vienna with a commission from Berlin to compose 12 quartets and sonatas. Soon he also started working on another opera, *Cosi Fan Tutte* (All Women Behave Thus). Despite the usual "snakes in the grass," the opera was a success.

Troubled Times

Even with the comfort of his music, Mozart was depressed and lonely. Constanze was usually away in the country, recovering from one illness or another. Their son Karl was in boarding school, which was a big expense. Another baby girl was born, but the child died right away.

Another blow was struck when Emperor Joseph II died in February 1791. All the court appointments were ended until the new emperor had decided which people to keep on. Mozart was hopeful, but very worried. His nights were spent tossing and turning. In the daytime he was too tired and depressed to do very much composing.

The coronation of the new emperor, Leopold II, was to take place in Frankfurt. The court composer, Salieri, could choose 15 musicians to perform at the ceremonies. Of course, hating Mozart as he did, Salieri overlooked him. But Mozart decided to go anyway, on his own. He pawned the last of his silver to buy a carriage for the trip.

Going to Frankfurt proved to be a costly mistake. Mozart gave a concert there, but received no money for it. Then he went on to Mannheim, where he'd been so warmly accepted in the past. Ten years had passed since he'd been in Mannheim, though. No one recognized him, and no one asked him to give a concert.

Discouraged, Mozart returned to his home. There he found two invitations to perform in London. Here was some good news for a change! Before he could go to London, though, he had to finish an opera he'd been working on. It was called *Die Zauberflöte* (The Magic Flute). The story was of a hero who could get through all sorts of danger as long as he had his magic flute in his hands. Mozart was nervous about the opera. After suffering so many disappointments, he was losing his confidence. He feared the opera would be a flop.

Other worries were on his mind as well. Constanze was sick again—and expecting a baby. Mozart himself was not feeling very well. Lack of money was, as always, a big concern. In July, at least one of his fears was taken away. Constanze delivered a healthy baby boy. They named him Franz.

6 CHAPTER
THE WORLD'S LOSS

"I have lost my beloved husband,
who cannot be forgotten by me
and all of Europe."

—Constanze Mozart
on her husband's death

Stranger
at the door

One day, shortly after Franz was born, Mozart was hard at work in his home in Vienna. It was very hot, and he was feeling a little dizzy. Suddenly he was startled by a knock on the door. "Come in!" Mozart called out weakly. A tall, gaunt stranger, dressed in dark gray, entered the room. He handed Mozart an anonymous letter. It was a request for Mozart to write a requiem (music for a funeral). He would be paid very well for composing the piece. But there was one condition. Mozart must never try to find out who the request was from.

This was very disturbing, but Mozart needed the money too badly to turn down the job. As his health grew worse, he became convinced that the requiem was for him. He feared his own death was near.

In reality, the request for the requiem came from a nobleman who was an amateur musician. This nobleman often passed off other composers' music as his own. Now his wife had died, and he wanted the requiem for her. If only Mozart had known the truth!

Hardly sleeping, living on medicine, Mozart hung on. Before he could start work on the requiem, he had to finish his new opera. He wrote the last notes of *The Magic Flute* on September 29, and the premiere took place on the very next night. The people of Vienna loved it.

Mozart's heart lightened. Maybe the future wasn't as bleak as he had thought. Although Constanze was back at the country health resort, Mozart became cheerful again. He wrote her long, joke-filled letters. When Constanze returned in November, however, she saw right away that her husband was very sick. She tried to keep him from working too hard. Telling him funny little stories, she did her best to boost his spirits.

Despite her efforts, Mozart didn't improve. He started having fainting spells. Once more, he became convinced that the requiem he was working on was for him. He thought his health problems were the result of being poisoned by one of his enemies. He even named Salieri as the person he suspected. Of course, Salieri was horrified by this story. He may have disliked Mozart, but he was no murderer! The accusation haunted him the rest of his life. Years later, on his deathbed, Salieri told a friend, "I did not poison Mozart."

At first, Constanze couldn't understand why Mozart was so upset about the requiem. "Don't you understand, Stanze?" Mozart asked. "I'm writing this piece for myself!" But Constanze refused to believe him. "Oh, Wolfi!" she cried. "Don't say such dreadful things!"

Then one day Mozart collapsed. His hands and feet were so swollen that he couldn't walk. He could no longer bear the chirping of his pet bird. "Take Starl away, please," he whispered sadly. Yet even as he sat in bed, he tried to finish the requiem.

Never Forgotten

Weak as he was, Mozart still enjoyed company. His friends came by often, filling him in on what was happening in Vienna's musical scene. On December 4, everyone gathered around Mozart's bed to sing parts from the still-unfinished requiem.

But Mozart was growing weaker and weaker. And at 55 minutes past midnight, December 5, 1791, he turned his face to the wall and died.

The news spread quickly throughout Vienna. In groups of two or three, people stood before his house and wept. The funeral itself was very small. Constanze couldn't even attend. At that time, women weren't allowed at funeral processions.

Mozart was buried in a common pauper's grave, with no witnesses. No cross was put on the grave. To this day, no one knows where his body lies.

In her grief, Constanze said, "I have lost my beloved husband Wolfgang, who cannot be forgotten by me and all of Europe." Today we know that the entire world will never forget Wolfgang Amadeus Mozart.

GLOSSARY

accompany—to play a musical part that adds to the main part, such as playing the piano for a singer.

aria—a melody sung by a single voice.

aristocratic—having to do with the upper classes.

city-state—a self-governing area made up of a city and the surrounding territory.

clavier—an instrument with a keyboard. When a key is pressed, a small hammer hits a string, which makes the sound.

coach—a horse-drawn vehicle; same as carriage.

commission—a fee paid for performing a service.

composition—a written piece of music.

concerto—a musical composition for one or more soloists and orchestra, made up of three separate parts.

conductor—person who directs a musical performance.

conservatory—a school for studying music.

coronation—the crowning of an emperor or king.

elector—a German prince who had the right to help choose the Holy Roman Emperor.

encore—a demand by an audience for a repeat of a work.

ensemble—a group of musicians playing two or more parts.

epidemic—a rapid spread of disease among a population.

genius—person with remarkable talent.

improvise—to do something without practice or planning; making up music as it is played.

leave of absence—taking a long time off from work with the employer's approval.

GLOSSARY

Lent—the time from Ash Wednesday to Easter. During this time, Roman Catholics and other churches take part in fasting and penitence.

libretto—the text or story of an opera.

minuet—a special type of music for dancing.

monastery—the home of people who have taken religious vows and live apart from the rest of the world.

musicales—a social gathering with music as the main entertainment.

opera—a play set to music, with singing and an orchestra.

oratorio—a long choral work, usually of a religious nature.

overture—an introduction or first part of a musical work, played by an orchestra.

patron—a wealthy person who supports a musician, writer or artist.

pauper—a very poor person who receives charity from the government or other people.

prodigy—a remarkably talented child.

register—a book containing public records.

requiem—a musical piece honoring the dead.

sonata—a musical piece for instruments, made up of three or four separate parts.

spire—a tall, pointed roof of a building; steeple.

symphony—a long, difficult musical piece performed by an orchestra.

third—two musical notes that are a third of a tone apart and sound pleasing when played together.

INDEX

LISTENING CHOICES

Operas
The Marriage of Figaro
The Magic Flute
Don Giovanni

Symphonies
Symphony in E Flat Major
Symphony in G Minor
Symphony in C Major *(Jupiter)*

Concerti
Concerto in C Major for Flute and Harp
Bassoon Concerto in B Flat Major
Piano Concerto in D Minor

Church Music
Requiem (unfinished)
Exultate

Chamber Music
Haydn Quartets for Strings
String quintet in G minor
The Flute Quartets

Other works
Piano Sonata in A Major
Eine Kleine Nachtmusik ("A Little Night Music")
Serenade in B Flat